KU-576-677

Golden Advices from Rumi

kozmik

GOLDEN ADVICES from RUMI

Edited by Ziya Elitez

Translation: Roni Rodrigue

First Printing: December 2005

ISBN: 975-8973-35-5

© Kozmik Kitaplar

All rights reserved. No part of this book may be reproduced in
any form or by any means without the prior written consent of the
publisher, excepting brief quotes used in reviews.

KOZMİK KİTAPLAR
Büyükdere Cad. Tevfik Erdönmez Sok.
Diker Apt. No: 26/5 Esentepe-İSTANBUL/TURKEY
Tel: +90 212 273 22 34 Fax: +90 212 273 25 19
info@kozmikkitaplar.com.tr

Golden Advices from Rumi

Edited by Ziya Elitez

Translation: Roni Rodrigue

I dedicate this book to my mother and father, with all my heart and sincere feelings, who helped me to achieve everything up to this day.

MEVLANA MUHAMMED
CELALEDDIN RUMI

The great Turkish Muslim poet and spiritual thinker Rumi was born in September 30, 1207 in today's Afghan city of Belh-Horasan.

His father, Bahaddin Veled, was one of the greatest thinkers' in Belh, and a *soufi* of the Melamatian philosophy. (Bahattin Veled's father, Huseyin Hatibi was also a great religious thinker) Rumi's father Veled was so respected because of his vast knowledge that he was renowned as the Sultan of the Scholars (*sultan-ul ulema*). Rumi's mother Mumine Hatun was the daughter of Rukneddin, the *Emir* of Belh.

Though married to a royal woman, Bahattin Veled did not get on well with the rulers of the period. Islamic principles were obeyed to in its strictest forms in Belh, during that era. He was always confronting these people in his classes and discussions, who tried to comply with the harshest terms of Islam but who in fact were so drifted away of Islam. He was constantly in opposition with the intolerations of those. Thus, making the excuse of the upcoming Mongol occupation, Veled decided to leave Belh together with his family and other closeby relatives in 1212 (According to other sources in 1218).

During this migration period to Anatolia over Persia, *Rumi*, his father being his first teacher, got the chance to meet the most respectable *sufis* of those times, like Ferideddin-i Attar, Shihabeddin Suhreverdi, Muhyiddin-i Arabi. They reached Anatolia in 1222 and settled in Larende's religious school, *medrese*, built by *Subasi* Amr Musa (today the town is known as Karaman). In this town, *Rumi* married to Cevher Banu, the daughter of Sherefeddin Lala in 1225 and they had two sons; Sultan Veled and Alaaddin Celebi. *Rumi*'s mother, Mumine Hatun and his son, Sultan Veled, who established the Mevlevian philosophy died here.

In 1228, the family moved to Konya, the capital city of the Anatolian Selchuk's, with the order of Sultan, Alaaddin Keykubat. They resettled in the *medrese* of Altunapa (Iplikchi). Konya was the cultural center of Anatolia at that time. Being the capital and also because of the previous migrations of Christians, the city was full of palaces, *medreses* and magnificient buildings. This situation attracted many famous artists, philosophers and scientists to Konya. The city was also a paradise for the famous Eastern scientists and artists running away from the Mongols; this also is one of the reasons for Islam to be known by the West. The cosmopolitan composure of the capital, Konya, brought together people speaking Greek, Hebrew, Turkish and Persian and was the cornerstone of *Rumi*'s vast and endless tolerance.

Rumi's father Bahattin Veled became famous, as a reliable, thrustworthy man and a good preacher soon after they arrived to Konya.

He lectured in religious schools (*medrese*) and educated a lot of students. *Rumi* also attended his classes. After his father's death in 1231 he continued his studies in mystic thoughts as a student of *dervish* Seyyid Burhaneddin Muhakkik, the latter being a student of *Rumi*'s father, himself. With Burhaneddin's advice he went to Aleppo and Damascus for further, deeper education. This period continued for seven years, during which time he was in contact with the most famous *dervishes* and *sufis* of that era. He was debating, exhanging ideas with them all the time. Because of his endless desire together with his father's and Seyyid Burhaneddin's supports, he read and studied Arabian, Indian and Greek philosophers' works. Due to his vast knowledge, he was loved and respected by everyone soon.

Thus he started to teach in religious schools (*medrese*), attracting the curiosity of many.

One day, after finishing his lessons in *medrese*, someone attracted his attention while he was going home. (This coincidance took place in October 1244 according to some and November 1244 according to other sources.) After an interesting discussion with Shemseddin Tebrizi, Rumi's life totally changed. Unknown to which religious sect he belonged to, Tebrizi was a Turkish *dervish* who had travelled in Iran, Iraq, Syria and Anatolia extensively. Tebrizi, well built and tall, wearing strange outfits, used to talk hard and agresively.

(One of Tebrizi's outfits is in the Konya Rumi Museum today) Tebrizi had his own ideas. After travelling so many places, he finally came to Konya. Shemseddin Tebrizi's way of thinking affected Rumi deeply. After their coincidental meeting they became really close friends, talking and discussing with each other all the time. Rumi mentioned his admiration and respect to Tebrizi in the poems he wrote during those days. (*"Let me die if I have a head other than you. Burn me if I live without you. You are my beloved in Kabe and in church as well. The fire of my love is over everything. I cannot hide Shemseddin' face in all this fire."*) Rumi, after all his discussions and talks with Tebrizi, understood that all that he knew and learned were tools in *Allah's* way. 6 months after he met Tebrizi, Rumi's other close friends and followers got irritated because of their relation.

Rumi had closed his school (*medrese*) and started to ignore his family, friends and students. Beause of this, many, started to oppose Shemseddin Tebrizi. Rumi's youngest son Alaaddin organised a group against Tebrizi in order to break his friendship with his father. They were thinking that they could not benefit from Rumi's ideas and love sufficiently any more. At the end, Tebrizi left Konya one night without informing Rumi. But this caused Rumi to contract within himself more. It is during this period that he started to his deep meditational transes. He wrote poems about brake aparts and was less and less in contact with people around him. Rumi constantly talked about and nothing else. Rumi's oldest son, Sultan Veled (who, in fact, knew Tebrizi very well and was very pleased with his and his father's debates and discussions and often took part in those discussions) went to Damascus to find Tebrizi. After finding Tebrizi, Veled made him come back to Konya. Shemseddin was greeted in Konya with a big ceremony, Rumi leading it.

After his return, Rumi became attached to Tebrizi more. Which irritated Rumi's friends deeper as well. When, Rumi fixed the marriage of a young girl who, his son Alaaddin loved, with Tebrizi, Alaaddin got furious. One night his son, Alaaddin Chelebi, with his friends killed Shemseddin Tebrizi. When the oldest son Veled learned about this, he took out Tebrizi's corpse from the well he was thrown in and buried him to a garden. He did not want his father to know. (It is also told that Tebrizi was very upset from all this, and that he left the town without letting anybody know to where he left.) This disappearence affected Rumi seriously. He went to Damascus twice hoping to find Shemseddin, but returned back to Konya frustrated and deeply upset.

After days without Tebrizi, he met a simple jeweller called Selahaddin Feridun. He gave the same friendship to Feridun as Tebrizi. The people close to Rumi again started to get dissatisfied with this situation. But this close friendship lasted for ten years, until 1259 when Feridun died. After Feridun's death, Rumi having reached to a high level of maturity, he met Celebi Husamettin, a *soufi* Turk.

(The name Celebi was given to Husamettin by Rumi.) Husamettin's father was also a *soufi* peer. They were called *Ahis*. This mystical friendship between Rumi and Husamettin caused the *Ahis* to be affected by Mevlevite way of thinking.

It is known that Celebi Husamettin affected Rumi while the latter was writing Mesnevi. Chelebi's constant persistance forced Rumi to write this magnificient masterpiece. The friendship between them, (which continued for 15 years) until Rumi's death did not disturb Rumi's followers this time. As Rumi's fame grew bigger and bigger, many known thinkers and philosophers of the time came to Rumi.

He got sick. Believing that dying is the rebirth, Rumi died on December 17, 1273, in Konya.

PREFACE

FROM THE OCEAN OF *RUMI*...

Rumi (Sept.30, 1207 Belh-Dec.17, 1273 Konya) is an incomparable artist, a great spiritual scholar. His poetical works, *Mesnevi and Divan-i Kebir* consist of thousands of verses. *Rumi* has five masterpieces. *Mesnevi* consisting of 6 volumes; *Divan-i Kebir* containing his *eulogies, ghazels, rubais* and poems; *Fihi Mafih*, in which his spiritual ideas are laid out in 61 parts; *Mecalis-i Seb'a* containing his 7 lectures; and *Mektubat* which consists of 150 letters.

Rumi is a teacher of souls. *Mesnevi*, shows men the true love, how to be an examplery person, with good ethics, honesty, generosity, humbleness, patiance, thrustworthyness, truthfullness by way of hundreds of stories. One has to take lessons out of these.

Rumi's spiritualism is good moral and ethical values. *Divan-i Kebir* contains 21 *divans* made up of *ghazels, eulogies, rubais and poems*. One can see his world of senses clearly; in his *ghazels* he explains the devine love. His 1725 *rubais*, translated by Adulbaki Gölpınarlı are collected in the book, named *Divan-i Rubaiyyat*.

In *Rumi's* spiritualism, the meaning of life and creation is love. His book, *Fihi Mafih*, with a total of 61 parts, contains his lectures and speaches done in public. This book explains his ideas on spiritualism, poetry, the real world and the spiritual world, heaven and hell, man, religion, belief and love.

In *Rumi's* spiritualism the aim is servitude and simplicity. Mecalis-*i Seb'a* contains his 7 lectures. The true richness is not being rich moneywise but to achive a soul richness. The true lovers of God are free of pride, greed and grudge, and with their common senses are freed from inattention and directed towards true belief. They are cleared from excesses and show offs; they are the true believers of justice and the beloved followers of God.

In *Rumi's* spiritualism the real aim is to reach to the owner of the soul and be the core. His work named *Mektubat* contains his 150 letters, written to different people. These letters are made up of stories, poems and verses from Quoran. They are divided into three: advices to man working for the government, helping those in need and answering questions asked to him on religious and scientific subjects.

Rumi's most obvious speciality is his tolerance. He never liked one to be hurt because of himself; he preferred not to answer a question from one who was thinking contrary to him, and thus make that person ashamed of his ideas. *If your friends tell you about their wrongs, say that "he knows the secret to this" and close the subject so that you are not left without a friend, in this world; because their is no friend who is faultless.*

Rumi's other virtues are modesty, being free of pride and arrogance and having his ideas consisting of simplicity. Being the *Sultan of Soules* is another virtue of him.

Rumi showed his generosity by not showing any consideration to worldly pleasures and possessions. When he was given a present he passed them on to poors; when he helped those in need he did that in such a way so that those people were not offended or ashamed and not letting others know that those people were aided.

In *Rumi's* spiritualism the aim is servitude and simplicity.

In *Rumi's* spiritualism the meaning of creation and life is love.

In *Rumi's* spiritualism the real aim is to reach to the owner of the soul and be the core.

Being an accomplished follower, *Rumi's* spiritual work is in accordance with the creation, to help men in reaching spiritul perfection and happiness.

Rumi's spiritualism is good moral and ethical values.

Rumi considers man as a very valuable being. *The aim of the universe is man (Mecalis-i Seb'a, p: 45).*

Rumi underlines this superiority of man in his works; he ordered *"there is a life within your life, search that life...but not on the outside, search it in yourself." (Rubais 22)*

Rumi divides creatures into three: angels, animals and humans. Angels are only intelligence; obeying, praying and serving are in their nature. Animals do not posses any intelligence but only passion. Only humans have to get rid of the bad values that are a burden for him: to long for lust and greed for a longer life, like a crow. These attitudes that are the barriers of wisdom prevent humanity reaching higher values.

All of *Rumi's* works are about love. Love is the meaning of life, the core, the reason of creation of the universe. Starting from this point of view he talked about holy love in thousands of his verses. The value and superiority of love, the poverty of those that is far apart from love's benefit.

In *Rumi's* spiritualism one cannot comprehend the metaphysical realities by knowledge and wisdom. These will lead man to certain levels, but not to the real aim. If man had wings of love, he could rise to levels that knowledge and wisdom cannot even dream about.

According to *Rumi* only the soul, that is attached to the loved one, to God, is considerable. Man can not reach God by wisdom, and will tumble half way. If the distance between man and God is a sea's length, wisdom is not enough for the journey; man will be tired while swimming, but one will reach his aim if he is on a boat.

According to *Rumi*, the sun is the proof of the sun itself. He ordered, *if you need proof, do not turn your face away from the sun* (Mesnevi 1/117). One's whose clothes are torn apart because of love, is purified from greed and mistakes; he ordered that love is the medicine of pride and the doctor of all illnesses (Mesnevi 1/22).

According to *Rumi*; man learns art in order to earn his daily living. He has to learn a craftsmanship for the other world as well. He adviced that this art of religion is also love (Mesnevi 2/2618).

According to *Rumi*; love other than love of God is not real love. If love is related to colour and odour, that is not love, it is a shame for man (Mesnevi 1/214).

Rumi finds the nature of creation and the uprising from man's worldly form, in love; life without love cannot be called life. Do not say, "I do not have the potential for this love." According to *Rumi*; one who is in love with the total will not credit the tiny. One who turns to tiny does not deserve the total (Mesnevi 1/2903).

Rumi says that we have to understand the real meaning and aim of the stories told in *Mesnevi*, not what we read in that great work.

"The aim is to take lesson in short, not to tell you stories" (Mesnevi 1/108).

According to *Rumi*; this world, which is an examination, ground where, everyone that truly burned up with God's love, passed from the same path. These paths are, at the same time, filled up with difficulties, pains and hardships. Everybody has the same aim.

Rumi, *with Mesnevi* gives messages to those who are in a true love with God; he shows the way, tells them that they are not alone along this path and acts as a guide to those.

According to *Rumi; a body that belongs to soil, remains on the ground, but the soil is the ordinance of the holy skies* (Mesnevi 2/3811). Man, wherever he is, whatever he looks like; if he possesses love of God, his value is higher than the skies.

According to *Rumi; like a mirror which can not reflect images when dust covers it, a soul which is covered with worldly faults will not be able to get God's justice.* For that reason, *the soul must be kept clean, must be filled with sincerety and love;* one must keep away from feelings like grudge and greed. He declared that *God does not care about how you look like and what you possess; he cares only about your souls and intentions. The souls of the holy, is the praying altar of the clean people* (Mesnevi 2/31). *A soul filled with love of God, reflect the light of God's sun* (Mesnevi 1/35). *A healthy soul is the liberator of a friend's intimacy.* (Mesnevi 2 / 1329).

According to *Rumi;* wisdom is divided into two: minute wisdom, total wisdom. Minute wisdom is form an; always needs to learn more. The total wisdom is for the creative power; everything that is active on this world is a shadow of the total wisdom. Wisdom, in comparison with love always sides with the superiority of love.

According to *Rumi; the* speciality about wisdom is that to think about the result. But self-esteem never thinks about the result. If wisdom starts to win, self-esteem gets weaker.

A patient goes to see a doctor because of his common sense, wisdom tells him to do so; but this wisdom will not help the patient in his recovery.

Men's wisdom is different in everyone; like *the appearence of each beauty is different* (Mesnevi 3/1542). In some, wisdom is like a candle without giving any light. In some others, it shines like a star (Mesnevi 5/762). Knowledge and experience increase wisdom, this causes   people to get more experianced; but *superiority from creation, increases by working* (Mesnevi 3/1546).

Therefore, since a medicine's effectiveness is hidden in itself, the meaning of everything one can see, is hidden in it (Mesnevi 4/2900).

According to *Rumi* both good and bad develops from you. *The ugly and the beautiful is what you gain with your own hands* (Mesnevi 3/3458). Life becomes eternal by believing. *If your companion is belief you are immortal* (Mesnevi 3/3311). For death he told that; "To live forever love forever; die with love so that you will stay alive!" (Rubais 181)

According to *Rumi;* man cannot have the real knowledge with his minute wisdom and personal opinions. Everyone has different opinions. Since there can only be one truth, everyone has different views and see the truth from different angles, one will not see the truth as a whole and will surely get mistaken.

According to *Rumi;* wisdom is like the seal of King Solomon. *World is a copy, and wisdom is its life; humanity gains dignity with wisdom* (Mesnevi 1/1071). *Love of God can be obtained by wisdom. Those that do not know this wisdom and the dumbs are drifted away from this love* (Mesnevi 2/1545). *Wisdom is the guide of man. Man, with his wisdom is superior to any other being* (Mesnevi 2/3361).

According to *Rumi;* knowledge is not the aim, it is a total that will lead man to God. "One who knows his self esteem knows God".

The meaning of this is, man has to realize from where he comes and where he is going.

According to *Rumi*; the *aim is leading man to a path. The path is that path, which its traveller becomes the king* (Mesnevi 2/3237).

According to *Rumi*; wisdom, which does not lead man to reality, which does not teach how to obey to its creator is a tool that is tiring. Wisdom should be a lover to its owner, not a burden. He accepts the wisdom in one's soul as the person's friend; and the things in the open as his burden (Mesnevi 1/2552). It is not enough to be wise (Fihi Mafih, p: 93).

According to *Rumi*; no one trusts a liar's swears, and a truthful person does not need swearing (Mesnevi 2/2902). Because living *awakens suspicion in souls and right words give tranquility to hearts* (Mesnevi 2/2762).

According to *Rumi*; modesty is a virtue that lifts its owner (Mesnevi 3/457).

According to *Rumi*; patience *is the key to comfort*. With patience all the hardships can be eliminated (Mesnevi 3/1848).

According to *Rumi*; *one who controls his rage will be protected from God's anger* (Mesnevi 4/114).

As mentioned in his eighteenth *couplet* of *Mesnevi*; "Words get longer, they must be cut!" An ocean, a brain resisting time, and a personality that could not be eroded with time, *Rumi* cannot be described totally with words. I saw that everybody compiled and commented about *Rumi's rubais, ghazels* and poems but not his famous words and idioms. I am really the first one to do so. After me, it is for sure that a better, an excellent and a best compilation will be done. The speciality of this work is it that it is a beginning. I would like to thank the following in helping me prepare this work:

- **ABDÜSSETTAR YARAR**
Konya City Cultur and Tourism Manager.
- **FAHRİ ŞAHİN**
Konya City Cultural Management, Cultur and Social Works Department.
- **DR. ERDOĞAN EROL**
Manager of the Mevlana Museum.
- **DR.NACİ BAKIRCI**
Ass. Manager of the Mevlana Museum.
- **MUAFAK ÖZSOY**
Konya City Special Administration Manager.
- **SÜLEYMAN SAYAN**
Konya Metropolitan Municipality Special Works Manager.
- **ALİ BEKTAŞ**
Konya Metropolitan Municipality Cultural Management.
- **MÜMİN TEMİZYÜREK**
Konya Metropolitan Municipality Cultural Management.
- **MEHMET BİREKUL**
Konya Metropolitan Municipality Cultural Management.

Ziya Elitez
November 2004

SELECTED *RUBAIS* FROM RUMI

Reach to being by nothingness, leave the world
If your path is reaching the other world, leave aside worldly goods,
If it is God your desire do not think deep,
Forget the world, reality, leave the meaning.

...

How many times did I ask to my peer at night?
"Tell me the secret of the world, quickly."
Smiling replied my peer;
"That, it is known, can not be told."

...

It is the same for me, the raisin-wine yards,
Love pulls me to four corners.
I return to truth, but not to Your surroundings,
Look, it is my surroundings that I return!

...

Suddenly that beauty entered through my door,
That beauty drank wine, stood for a moment.
To watch and hold her hair,
My face became totally eye, my eye hand.

...

I cannot pull my hand, from secrets for long,
To talk and open there is no possibility.
The secret that will please you lies in me;
If I can say, but there is no possibility.

...

I reached my peer one day, while in total pleasure,
Said; "What is to be, what is to be nothing?"
"Stay like that, stay away from the guilts of people,"
To be and to be nothing is a curtain for men.

...

It is always Him, to be or to be nohing, pleasure and sadness,
Whatever the desire, it is always Him that creates from nothing.
Oh if ever you had an eye in you to see you,
You are Him, know that, the Holy fate is like this!

...

My love is secret from the entire universe.
Is in disguise from emotion, from every kind of suspicion.
It is in my soul like a moon,
It is life and flesh, flesh and life is secret.

...

Is it me, me, is it you, you, is it me, you?
Is it me, you are definately you, and you, me.
Oh generous love, I am so pleased with you,
Is it you, me or is it me, you, be not suspicious.

...

So destroyed we are, try to vanish again!
Do not give any sorrow, try to play *rebab*!
With the beautiful odour my lover, becomes your atlar,
So many bending forward, try to pray!

...

The secret on four corners, the full moon, where are they? .
Where is, my beloved friend, the "hey" that is desired in life?
There, it is always possible to say, the universe is all Him,
A living eye is not possible to see Him, where is the "hey"?

...

Come and see my friend, I have thousands of flesh,
What can I do, how can I do, my mouth is sealed.
There are this much people, always saying "I", "me",
There is no one, saying only "I am you".

...

The seas are not sufficient for us, what can a river do?
Not desiring for a rose, its smell is worth a life.
My loved one can do mistakes, it is nice,
This patiance is special for us, whatever my loved does.

...

Please say my friend with mercy, that love is a good thing,
Yes, it will give damage to love if it increases, the wine.
You have named lust, love, what a pity,
When love is named, bow to this holy feeling!

...

Oh the loved one with tamed ways, those that see you are in love with you,
It flows out from every being and places.
It is not a star, nor moon, there is no sign of beauty,
The entire universe runs with loads of love to the sun's illumination.

...

Oh tired and waterless soul, look for a river;
Run, do not come without legs, sweat and blood, come like that!
Start your travel without tongue-mouth;
What is truth, say something and come!

...

The unique loved one does a sweet play to me,
"Is it single or double, whatever your desire, tell me immediately!"
Laughing, lets be double, come my beauty," I said,
"Lets be double and stay single, my loved, understand..."

...

If I could be a dream to the colours of this times,
If I could wow the smell of life, to loved one with tamed ways
If I could be my mirror, while watching Him,
If I could see Him, every moment watching me.

...

We are like many things rising from the same soul,
Inside two lives we are one, like reflecting to eternity we are.
There is certainly a beautiful meaning of our love;
Know that you in me and me in you, like a secret, each.

...

My loved bird did something good and skipped food,
Did something bravely and stopped from pleasure.
The loved, passed into my soul in a moment, holding out a friendly hand,
Bowed instantly to the loved and passed all these griefs.

...

I am the servant of that man; all this pleasure is beautiful and nice,
The sorrows of that man are mine; his soul is filled with loyalty.
Different taste, different odour, I have no other knowledge,
I am delighted with sorrows; in him hard times are like birth.

...

A day will come when so many pale faced men and women in apocalypse,
Are lined to be questioned, with screams and cries.
I will lay down your love on my lap with all my hands,
"Ask me if I have a guilt, the guilty is him," I say.

...

Stride and shut your eyes, your soul becomes so many lives,
So another world lightens to you in those eyes!
If you do not get proud of yourself being under the rule of your desires,
You can be a loved man, than you can give life!

...

Cry wholeheartedly, cry my friend, only the neighbour hears,
If a child cries deeply, it is the mother that wants.
The mother is free, to work and do the job, you keep crying,
Crying is the real worth my friend, say love and wake up!

...

That kingly *semah* gives us a different *semah* every night,
That rose field's wind blows differently.
So many nightingales, birds do not believe in this love of *semah*, but,
In this *semah* the branch, the tree blow towards a new love.

...

We are so happy with the loved, tonight,
Oh, how our soul gives us trouble,
Because of love we do roses, constantly,
Always planting for one sugar straw.

...

One that speaks with love, like leaves,
Keeps collecting earth and dust with eyebrows.
The love of nothingness blossoms everywhere,
A believer shouts out, sincerly: "You are one, the only One!"

...

"There are the lightning of justice in every climate "says again my friend
"Where is the light," people ask us, tell them my friend.
The eye tries to see, but a voice speaks up;
"Try to look for once without saying right or left, my friend!"

...

My friend calls, open your chest, your smile must end;
Get over from your times of pleasures, miseries!
Let the enemy build its spider web;
Only the tale bird knows the mountain in the tale.

...

Look my swaying love, so many traps,
Let them be for you; away from bad looks!
You are the life of earth, sky,
Let this peace be yours, be happy!

...

The day is over but we are the voice of happiness.
We are completely a subject of joy.
We are the lover and the loved of ourselves,
And of nightingales, rose gardens and everything.

...

My beloved, please stay even if everyone leaves!
My friend of hard times, sit and wait, do not go away!
Like rose-sugar fill my cup with fresh wine;
Here is everyone, leave your mark my beloved, do not leave!

...

You are waging a war, a horrible night facing you,
Throw an arrow from your soul; tear apart your dark surroundings!
You are the Holy Shrine of the lovers, pray everyday like that around it,
Let the Holy Shrine come to you with love and to pray around you!

...

How sweet is the *semah* today, how sweet it is, the *semah*,
The day is so full of light, the light is beautiful, and the light is pure.
This love is beautiful, deep, always deeper,
Goodbye to senses, this road is long, stay in peace!

...

For flesh the wine is banned, for man,
The flesh, frees itself from bondage, no ban is left.
Give us my good friend; do not tell us that there is no wine,
Even though we will drink constantly, it is fine!

THE FIRST 18 COUPLETS OF MESNEVI

Hear the constant complaints of this *ney*
This *ney* always tells about breaking apart.

Says, my cries are because of being a straw;
If anyone hears, blood will fall as tear drops.

A heart is torn to pieces because of breakin apart,
I want, I have to spill out my sorrows.

If ever the soul can part from itself a bit,
Stays like that, let time reach its destination.

Every where I cried, always with bitterness,
To every person that I saw, I said "my friend".

Everyone accepted me as a friend but,
No one asked for my secret.

My secret is not far away from my cry,
But there is no light in the eyes, the ear cannot hear.

The body-soul is obvious, see the human,
There is no permission, but the human cannot see, the soul.

The music of *ney* filled with air became fire,
Let him vanish, whoever lacks that fire!

Love became fire and spilled into *ney*,
The attraction of love is mixed into wine.

Ney made friend those other than the lover,
Our curtain is torn because of its sound.

The flute gives petition from a bloody way,
Always giving examples from the loves of mad one.

Ney is the poison and also the antidote, oh where is it,
A friend like that, a lover with such passion?

It is the secret of this mind, can not be known by mind,
A person is only a customer with one ear for the tongue.

Only pain, sorrow, so many days and nights are wasted,
The days passed on with mistakes, like that.

If the days pass on, there is no fear, everything is story,
Oh, the example of pureness, you stay do not leave!

Everthing believed only the fish does not believe anything other than water
The day gets longer, if the soul cannot get what it deserves.

Know that a humble person cannot realise a mature one,
The words are getting longer, it is time to stop!

GOLDEN ADVICES
from RUMI

Be like a river in generosity and giving help
Be like a sun in tenderness and pity
Be like night when covering others' faults
Be like a dead when furious and angry
Be like earth in modesty and humbleness
Be like a sea in tolerance
Be as you are or as you look like

How good it is to migrate every day
How beautiful it is to stop somewhere every day
How nice it is to flow without freezing and getting muddy
What word that belongs to yesterday,
Is gone my loved one, with yesterday,
Now is the time to say new things.

Come, come, and come come whatever you are!
Come if you are an atheist, if you are non believer,
if you believe in un-true Gods,
Our shrine
Is not a shrine of mishope?
Come again
Even if you have not kept your promises for thousand times...

What is for me in others' honey sherbet!
Here is my bowl of *ayran* in front of me,
I have no belongings or provisions,
I will stil work, for you to possess estates,
For you to have a place to cover your head
I am your tree.
BUT I WILL NEVER SELL
MY FREEDOM TO SERVITUDE
They are many by themselves
Like the almonds, those almonds.
But their oil is all the same.
So many languages on this world, so different languages,
But their meanings are all the same.
START BREAKING YOUR POTS, BOWLS,
HOW THE WATERS WILL FIND A WAY TO FLOW.

Is this possible, our souls unaware?
Me in you, you in me borning, hiding.
It is for me to describe you saying me, you
In truth we know there is no me, you between us.

Search in yourself, whatever you want!
There is another one in you, look for that one!
There is a treasure in your mountain, search for that treasure!
If you are looking for the walking *dervish;*
Do not search him outside of you,
Search him in your self-esteem!

My heart wants Him, everything else is pretence...

⊷⊶

Wherever I rest my head, He is bowed to.
In four corners and six towns, He is praised and honored.
Wine yards-gardens, roses-nightingales, heavens, loved ones;
All those are excuses; the real aim is He.

⊷⊶

The good ones have left.
Their good ways and attitudes are left behind;
And cruelty and loaths from the bad ones!

⊷⊶

Rape and Lust make one cross-eyed; separates Soul from the right
path...Tyrans' Tyranny is a dark well.

⊷⊶

If you did not look for your life's palace, that means you know:
You are what you search.

⊷⊶

Cover, so that your faults may be covered...

The value of the pouch and wisdom is the gold they possess. What value the pouch and wisdom has if they do not possess any gold.

┅━━┅

How blessed is he, whose companion is not envy.

┅━━┅

What is gold, what is life, pearl, coral are things, if not spent for a lover, not sacrificed for a beauty.

┅━━┅

I have not witnessed a better virtue and competence than good manners.

┅━━┅

I swear I do not even think about others' honey, if my bowl of *ayran* is in front of me. Hunger, even if it will cause my death,

┅━━┅

I never sell my freedom to servitudet!

┅━━┅

From whom are we running away, from ourselves? How impossible! From whom are we freeing, from God?
What a wasteless effort!

Whoever does not have a tendancy for Love, he is like a bird without wings, Pity on him!

⊹⫘⫘⊹

Lover gives flavour to all bitter things.

⊹⫘⫘⊹

Whatever there is in a jug leaks out.

⊹⫘⫘⊹

We are not one to be bribed,
Nor a king, mighty and rich;
We saw knitted souls broken to smitherens,
We mend them.

⊹⫘⫘⊹

Didn't I tell you not to go there;I am the only one who knows you, beckons you; in this illusion of nothingness. I am your only source.

⊹⫘⫘⊹

Even if you get angry, even if you go to roads lasting thousand years, you will come back to me again; it is only me where you will end.

Those words that you will say over my grave spill them to my grieving ears; tell them to me now.

⊹══⊱⊰══⊹

Rest…. We are like a compass. One foot lays firm over religious orders, while the other travels around all the nations.

⊹══⊱⊰══⊹

The value of the pouch and wisdom is the gold they possess.

What value the pouch and wisdom has if they do not possess any gold? Him that makes the rain pour from skies is able to give life with His mercy.

⊹══⊱⊰══⊹

God gave you life for free, that is why you do not value it. There is not one good that has become bad. Which roof did not collapse and lay on the ground? If knowledge is reflected to soul, for the good of humanity, than it is helpful but if it is reflected to flesh and things, than it is a burden, a catastrophy.

⊹══⊱⊰══⊹

Oh one that builds a well with tyranny! You are preparing your own trap. Oh, the eye that weeps for others! Come and weep for yourself for a little while! Candle, brightens more by crying.

The Lord, created thousands of chemicals, medicines; but humanity have not seen chemistry like patiance.

⊹⇌⊹

How much of the sea you can fill into a bowl? Luck for a day! The eye brows of the greedy do not fill up; instead if not satisfied, it will not be filled with pearls.

⊹⇌⊹

An animal gets heavier with grass, a person develops with honour. Know that heart that is sided with bad behaviour is not worth a dime. Love has such a force that, it burns everything over than the loved.

⊹⇌⊹

Hundred men can sit around a dining table, and eat. But, world is not enough for two men who want to be in the lead.

⊹⇌⊹

After us, it is the Mesnevi who will be the *sheik* and will show the right path to those searching it, and will lead them.

Semah is the food of the lovers; because in *Semah* there is the dream of reaching God. With the gown and cap you cannot be a wise man. Wisdom is a virtue in a person's self. This virtue can be like a dress in silk or wool.

⊹╾═╼⊹

God is closer to one than his main vein. On the contrary, you are firing your thoughts to places far away. Oh, one that takes out his arrow and throws it! The hunted is near you, you are searching far away.

⊹╾═╼⊹

One cannot see everything; those things that you love, make you blind and deaf.

⊹╾═╼⊹

The aim of a book is the knowledge inside; but if you want, you can use it as a pillow under your head. This is as if you stuck a sword to a wall like a nail and accepts loosing from the start.

⊹╾═╼⊹

There are so many lays in their tombs with better and brighter usefulness, and illuminance than hundreds of living.

Dead and hiding his shadow; but his ground giving out his shadow. They say, an idea should open a road. They say, a road, should meet a king. They say, a king, should be a king himself and not with fortunes and soldiers. Which bucket is lowered to a well and did not come up full; why should life shout from the well? When you close your mouth on this side, open it on the other side; from now on your miseries, is on the way of your homelessness.

⋆⋲⋗⋆

I was dead, I am reborn; I was the cry, I became laughs; nation of love arrived; I became an everlasting nation.

I have one soul, a courageous heart; I have the guts of a lion; I became a star, newly born and shining.

⋆⋲⋗⋆

As long as life is in my flesh, I am the slave of Qouran. I am the ground under the path of God's elite prophet Mohammed.

Whoever says something from me other than this, he will really cause my sadness.

⋆⋲⋗⋆

Pain allways adds up to more pain. How can a foul word be equal to a right one?

The eye that sees the sea is different than an eye that sees the bubbles...Try to look with an eye that sees the sea, not the bubbles. Day and night, bubbles are madeup of sea, and it is the sea that activates them. But it is amazing that, YOU SEE THE BUBBLES, NOT THE SEA.

Leave aside all the worldly things along this road. Do not move until your guide moves. One that moves without a head becomes tail. The move of this kind of a man, is like the move of a scorpion.

Respect is right; but a man's work is right as well! Come to your senses and do not be blind like a devil.

Look for the guilt in yourself; you planted the seeds. Make peace with God's law and punishment! The reason of trouble is doing something wrong. Look for the wrong in what you do; do not say, "this is my fate".

When a flood starts to act like a flood and flows down roaring try to stop it at the beginning; otherwise it will demolish and ruin everything on its way.

The Allmighty promised to give, on the other side, what we deserve about our rights and wrongs, but on this world, in every breath and vision we have His example. A joy to a man's soul is because he gave joy to another. He is gloomy because he made gloomy and sad another. These are the prizes of the other side; punishment will show you the way; these litlle things all tell that big thing; as if showing a handful of wheat in a wheat barn, just like that.

⊱━━⊰

It is not right to break a poor man's heart. God ordered "do not underestimate a fatherless; do not turn away emptyhanded, one that asked for". The wall said to the nail, "Why are you drilling me, hurting me?" And the nail replied, "Look who pins me!"

⊱━━⊰

Oh God! Show the gren branches of the holy tree, to the bird of life leaving the cage of flesh to be desired in time of death; so that with that desire it can move its wings fearlessly and can fly from its cage with joy.

⊱━━⊰

Boil, not to go wrong...Walk, to be as illuminating as Burhan-i Muhakkik. If you are freed from yourself, you will be Burhan totally. If you be a servant and disappear, you will be a king.

One who wants to stay with God, should seat with the holies. If you are drifted from the presence of the holies you are lost.

Because you are little within the whole. If thanking is making faces, no one appreciates the vineager.

Beware of gloomy thoughts. The heart of a man is like a bush and a forest. You can find ideas like a lion as well as a wild mule.

Why do we ask politeness from the mighty God? Because, rude people spared from God's mercy. A rude person, not only does wrong to himself, but he fires the horizons of shame and virtue.

For God one can throw himself into fire. But before jumping, search if there is holiness in you. Because fire recognizes not you, but the holy and will not burn them.

A warped shoe fits onto a warped foot.

Do not go to the village of hopelessness; there are hopes,
Do not walk towards dark; there are Suns.

Any person's conciousness bleeds when he does not perform his duty in full and neither excuses nor medicines can be of help.

Before death takes what is given, everything that has to be given must be done.

＋＝＝＋

I learned solitude from those that I have been with. Diets are really the basis of medicine; make diet, so that you can watch the strength and power in your soul.

＋＝＝＋

You are digging a well with cruelty, but know that you are digging that well for yourself. Do not knit around yourself like a silkworm; if you have to dig a well, dig it as deep as yourself.

＋＝＝＋

If the blacksmith is black, smoke cannot leave a mark on his face.

＋＝＝＋

A stone cannot become gren even though spring has passed,
Be earth and see how the roses blossom.
Enough, you were like a stone braking a lot of hearts,
Be earth, nice roses will blossom on you.
All the universe is connected to each other with love learn to give your love. Let your soul understand that, there is room for everything; the world is scared from one who hasn't got love.

If people were not mad about love they would not be able to reach perfectness.

One that gives advices by working is better than the one that gives advices with words.

Oh Mighty Mevlana, the rightious friend,
If you want to give light like the morning, you have to tame your passions that look like the night.

If a mind is coupled with another mind; the light has increased and the path has appeared. But if passion, is happy with another passion; the darkness increases, the path becomes flu.

I was raw, I boiled, and I burned.

A sharp sword cannot cut a soft silk.

Anger and desire makes one cross eyed; separates one's soul from the right way; virtue is covered when grudge gets in the way; hundreds of curtains from the soul are drawn in front of the eye.

✦══ ══✦

Know that unless you die, your agony won't stop. Because you didn't die before death your agony has gone on.

✦══ ══✦

You will not get anything wrong from this love my soul!
Do not be afraid if life is gone, death is another life.

✦══ ══✦

If you desire to find the friend in good times
Free yourself from what you look like, try to discover the core!
It is covered with many layers of sheet
He is within you; the universe is captive in Him.

✦══ ══✦

The outside of silver is white, bright but because of it the hands and clothes get dark. The fire has a red face, but look what a bad thing it does; watch the darkness at the end.

Oh the Clever! Never get drunk and be sorry for it when you get sober.

⊹╾╾╾⊹

The court is large but there are no brave men in it,
It is a time in which there are no familiar attitudes.
Everyone looks like a holy!
For Islam, there is no fire any light in soul.

⊹╾╾╾⊹

If you are completely in difficult times, if you are in hard times, be patient; because patiance is the key of good times.

⊹╾╾╾⊹

Look at the world we live in; the Mighty God, has grown all his creations in the lap of love. Why do we try to reach to our destination by hitting and kicking instead of caressing and hugging?

⊹╾╾╾⊹

The bitter things get sweet with love; copper gets gold with love; the residues become stable, clean with love; the miseries find help with love; the king becomes a regular man with love.

The colour of your eyes blinded me,
You called me and dismissed me, which one is right?
I will not be tricked with my lips getting wet,
Throw me into your river, the best thing is drawning me.

To persever someone's bad times, is a value that God Almighty likes, the Prophet loves and the holies desire.

A porter, who puts himself under a heavy weight, grabs all the weight from the others.

The promises of the elderly are a treasure that keeps moving on; the promises of those that are unworthy is a burden, a misery that keeps flawing.

Praise a good man, as you desire; those that keep their words are worth every good word.

Water always wins over fire. But if in a bowl, the fire boils that water and destroys it.

⊱━━⊰

Do not search for water! Be waterless, so that the water coming from up and dawn can inflame, boil.

⊱━━⊰

Passion that looks like fire won't decrease as long as it burns; it will decrease when you don't give in your desire.

Does a fire burn out, as long as you throw in wood? Does it not burn the fire?

You are made up of water; but you believe that you are the pot.

⊱━━⊰

This world looks like a tree; and we are like fruits on that tree, some ripe and some unripe.

⊱━━⊰

Recognize men well! Don't think that all are bad and humiliate them; also don't think that all are good and praise them.

Wish, miss; but wish and miss in a limit; a piece of straw cannot lift a mountain. The sun that illuminates the world, if it gets nearer a little bit will burn everything.

⸻

After our death do not search for our tomb on the ground! Our tomb is in the hearts of wise men.

⸻

There will be left nothing bad in you, if you look for good.

⸻

Unless the heart burns, the eye will not weep.

⸻

I was worrying that I did not have shoes on my way, I saw someone coming without his feet.

⸻

No one dies of being satisfied from what he has, no one becomes a king by feeding greed.

How rich you can be,
You can only eat as much as you can.
When you put the bucket in the sea,
It can fill up until it is full, the rest remains outside.

⊹═⟩⟨═⊹

We have to try to understand ourselves, before reading any book.

⊹═⟩⟨═⊹

We are all toys; power is his;
Richness is his, we are poor of course!
Why do we all look for pride in ourselves?
At the end everyone is the companion of a door.

⊹═⟩⟨═⊹

One can conquer the world but cannot conquer his words.

⊹═⟩⟨═⊹

One that plants the seeds of prickles; return to your senses, never search for it in the rose garden.

If you are with God, death and life are pleasent.

⊹═══⊱⊰═══⊹

Without depending and surrendering totally to God; good times and bad times are both traps, both illusions.

⊹═══⊱⊰═══⊹

Breaking is the mix of the one that mends he broken. One that saws, tears apart as well, whatever one sells, he buys something better.

⊹═══⊱⊰═══⊹

One that does not see his hand thinks the pen wrote it.

⊹═══⊱⊰═══⊹

Know that the figure seen will be destroyed; it is the spiritual world that is forever. Why do we have to play with the shape of the pot? Leave the shape of the pot aside, look for the water.

⊹═══⊱⊰═══⊹

Even if you get to high positions in life, you will still be agonized with the scare of loosing.

Win plenty of good things like a sea, but be a ship in it.

⊰━━⊱

Good talk and pity are humans' rage and lust is animals' virtues.

⊰━━⊱

Everything attracts another thing; heat attracts heat, cold attracts cold. Those who are false keep attracting false ones.

⊰━━⊱

Your being is your ideas,
The rest bones and flesh.

⊰━━⊱

Night gives birth to whatever it carries.

⊰━━⊱

Old men see on a brick more than what young men can see on a mirror.

⊰━━⊱

Can a hand perform anything secretly from the soul?

A man, whose hand is held by his soul, will not be drawn into the mud of his bad desires.

⊹━⊹━⊹

Unless you give your soul, you will not be able to find a soul.

Does a child release the smelly onion unless he sees the apple?

⊹━⊹━⊹

Peacock's enemy is its feet. There are so many kings that his power and strenght killed him.

⊹━⊹━⊹

The proof of the sun is the sun itself. Do not turn your face away from the sun if you are searching for a clue.

⊹━⊹━⊹

Whoever has a beauty, should know that's borrowed.

⊹━⊹━⊹

This dearly life passes away either trying to fill up our pockets with money or trying to eat and drink well, and the breath, which is numbered, decreases.

When the scarecrow starts to sing, the nightingales get silent.

※—※

The *kebab* of one, who is after the warrior lion, never diminishes.

※—※

A man has to leave many mansions to reach home one day.

※—※

To go visiting a friend barehanded is like going to the windmill without the wheat.

※—※

Leave greed aside; don't waste yourself for unworthy things,
The water is under the soil, and the apprentice in a master.

※—※

We said, be a shepherd, he became wolf. We said, be a guard, he became thief.

※—※

For years you were a stone that scratched souls; try to be the soil for a while.

When the shepherd sleeps, the wolf is sure of himself.

A wise person is the one that takes lesson from mistakes and deaths of his friends.

Even if he speaks hundreds of different languages, one is accepted as mute, if his heart and words are not the same.

With every breeze you sway like grass, you cannot touch grass if you are as high as a mountain.

To try to teach knowledge to a dumb man is like placing a sword in the hands of a bandit.

Medicine does not look for anything other than malice on this world.

Oh, one that throws the ore of belief for bread,
Oh, the poor man that sells the treasure for a bit of barley!
Nemrit, didn't surrender his soul to Abraham,
But surrendered his life to a mosquito.

Do not rest in believing. Unless being burned, you cannot reach to believe in what you see with your eyes. If the ear starts to see it will act like an eye; otherwise word will rest in the ear.

A man is valued by looking at what he looks for.

There are so many wise men, so many virtues that run in the front that, if man wants to become the leader with it, will loose his head. If you do not want to loose your head be the foot.

It is nice when friends come together; hold on to the skirts of morality; the things in view are stubborn and make the heads dizzy. Try to melt these stubborn things in view, with miseries so that you can watch the unity that is like a treasure, underneath that.

The pity and goodness of an illiterate is little.

✦━━✦

You are life, even though that is what you are, you think you are the body.

✦━━✦

A rude person is nicer in public than those that are not in public; the knob is bended as well, but it is still on the door.

✦━━✦

Question borns from knowledge, as well as the answer.

✦━━✦

One that spares the water beside the river is one that does not see the water.

✦━━✦

Do not sell mirror in the blind market; do not sing in the deaf market.

✦━━✦

A book is a letter sent to the future.

The sea does not get dirty because a dog's lip touched it.

⊹══⚬══⊹

Sorrows always show the one way.

⊹══⚬══⊹

There is always a corner in the soul of a man with sorrows that is full of mist and suspicion. If you listen him you open a window in that soul.

⊹══⚬══⊹

The true meaning of religion cannot be understood; it can only be admired.

⊹══⚬══⊹

Religion is a free heritage from your father; that is why you lifted your head and do not thank for it. Does a man who got a heritage know the value of his inheritance?

⊹══⚬══⊹

When a singer pauses does it not increase his voice?

In order to say a word, one has to hear and listen first. So, you start speaking by way of listening.

⊹⟞⟝⊹

Be friend with people. As much as the caravan is crowded with many people, the bandits are that much scared away.

⊹⟞⟝⊹

There are ways of praying, silent or loud; those that spill out from lips, those that blossom in the souls, they have holy shrines, praying carpets. But the holiest prayer, one that is blended with the life's prayer. Grudge and envy, greed and injustice, pride and prejudice, cannot get into this holy body and all the earth's dirt is washed, when the soul relaxes.

⊹⟞⟝⊹

Praying and worshipping is being with God. For one who is with God, life and deaths are both nice.

⊹⟞⟝⊹

A ship needs water to sail. But water; if it penetrates into the ship, it will sink the ship. What water means for a ship, world is for a believer.

World is like a magnet; attracts all the straws, only real wheat, can escape from its attraction.

⊹⊱══⊰⊹

If you think about a rose, you are a rose garden; if you think about prickle you are a wood, good for a fireplace.

⊹⊱══⊰⊹

Brother! You are made up of idea and thought. These are your existance. The rest is bone and nevre that exist in an animal as well.

⊹⊱══⊰⊹

A rude person does not harm only himself; sends fire all around. This sky is full of lights because of kindness; an angel is freed from guilt and gets cleaned because of kindness.

⊹⊱══⊰⊹

The difference between a human and an animal is kindness.

⊹⊱══⊰⊹

Greed and passion for worldly goods, gorce man to reach out for things that he does not deserve.

What is justice? To water the trees. What is tyranny? To water prickles. Justice is to place goodness to where it is deserved; not to water every seed that pulls the water. What is tyranny? Not to use one thing properly, to place it where it does not belong.

<hr>

Cry when one is born, not when one dies.

<hr>

When one weeps, it means that the sea of pity has erupted.

<hr>

Which river has entered into the soil and not flown out? Why are you suspicious of a believer?

<hr>

I searched the entire universe. I have not found a beter virtue than good manner.

<hr>

Good manner is what makes an illiterate person like an iron, more valuable than a genious like gold.

Mind, because it is mind sees the end of things; mind that does not see the end becomes passion.

⊹⊱══⊰⊹

A person becomes wise by using his mind, not by getting his beard and hair white.

⊹⊱══⊰⊹

To grab the hunt from your neighbours is a shame for the lions, not for dogs.

⊹⊱══⊰⊹

Look, the arrow is flying, the bow is hidden; lives are around while life for other lives is hidden.

⊹⊱══⊰⊹

Our tongue cannot be burned by fire...only him!
It is our aim that we lack... only him!
Cannot be talked about our hard times... only him!

⊹⊱══⊰⊹

There is aways a better than the existing one; since it is not the best it should not be loved. Free your soul from the idols you love; see the beauty without a form and shape.

He demolished the house for a treasure of gold; with that treasure he will build a stronger house.

⊹══ ══⊹

What do you have, what have you obtained? What kind of a pearl you took out from the sea? There will not be such a feeling in the day of death; does life have soul to be friend with yours? Earth will fill these eyes in the grave. Do you have light to illuminate even a blind's eye?

⊹══ ══⊹

How much you know; what you say is only as much as the listener can understand.

⊹══ ══⊹

To say right to everything is foolish; one that says everything is wrong is a tyrant.

⊹══ ══⊹

To search for something where it is not, means it is not searched for.

⊹══ ══⊹

Birds always fly with their own kind.

You have to pull your hands out of this world in order to be educated in the way of research. Try to cure this blindness in your eyes! Otherwise the universe is all Him, but there has to be an eye to see.

⊢⊣

Birds always fly with their own kind.

⊢⊣

Always try to run away from a bad friend; a bad friend is worst than the most poisinous snake; a snake by injecting its poison kills one; but a bad friend causes one to loose his life and beliefs.

⊢⊣

A stone cannot get green even after thousand spring times pass by.

⊢⊣

A lover looks like gold, trouble like fire. Pure gold is nice on fire.

⊢⊣

Only fire can burn out love.

⊢⊣

There is no compassion or suffering in love.

Love is not gold, cannot be hidden; there is no secret in a lover.

⊹≈≈⊹

Love is like a case, trouble is like a witness; if you do not have a witness, you will not win your case.

⊹≈≈⊹

Your love has surrounded me, advices are in vain; I drank that poison, this trouble is for nothing.

⊹≈≈⊹

At first looking at a higher being blinds your vision, but gives light to eyes, the illuminance is forgiving. Force your eyes to get used to the illuminance, if you are not a bat look at that side. To see the end of the work is the clue of your light.

⊹≈≈⊹

What wind means to fire, being separated is the same for love; will burn out little love, will strengthen big love?

⊹≈≈⊹

Break the coloured glasses that blind your eyes and look, so that you can understand what hits your eyes.

If you pull out water from the sea without replacing it, the sea will dry out and become a desert.

＊＝＝＊

Sadness is made up of wishes that will not become true.

＊＝＝＊

The tongue is like an endless treasure as well as an incurable illness.

＊＝＝＊

One whose tongue and words are not the same, even if he has hundred tongues, he is still mute.

＊＝＝＊

The biggest idol is your greed's idol.

＊＝＝＊

Do not free a donkey's head, keep hold of its reigns, because it likes to go to the grass.

＊＝＝＊

The rights ones do not need to swear.

There are stars even if the blinds cannot see.

+≔≕+

Keep visiting your friends. Because; roads that are not walked on will be covered with prickles and bushes.

+≔≕+

If you are looking for peace, be friendly, redeem quickly and do your work.

+≔≕+

Man is made up of core; the rest is skin.
The eye is, one that sees friend.

One, who has a good friend, does not need a mirror.

+≔≕+

Feelings are prisoners of the brain; brain is the prisoner of the soul.

+≔≕+

In order to see the world, a true eye is needed.

One who speaks without thinking is like a hunter who shoots without aiming.

⊹═══⊱

Not every prickle gives a rose.

⊹═══⊱

A candle does not loose its light by lighting another candle.

⊹═══⊱

Cats are masters of those with a rat's attitude.

⊹═══⊱

Whatever you write will be lost as long as your pen is of wind, your paper of water.

⊹═══⊱

The colour of your face has marks of your soul.

⊹═══⊱

The bent crow, if it knew how ugly it was, would have melted like snow because of its sorrow.

If one shoe is small to your foot, both are useless.

—————

Living or dead, every being is a book.

—————

The world consists of bold desires, like useless toys. And we are children.

—————

How can you get roses if you plant prickles? How can a plant give fruit if there is no soil? Your works are each a seed and the universe a windmill; if you go and put in a windmill what you have, you will bring it back by kicking.

—————

The roses' endurance to the prickle causes it to have a   beautiful smell.

—————

The soil will not let out its secrets until the God's springtime order arrives.

Tears, not water, can clean the dirt inside.

⊹══⊹

Winds, often blow in directions that ships do not desire.

⊹══⊹

Do net get used to bad things; they will be rooted, and stay forever.

⊹══⊹

The universe is connected to each other with love. Learn to give your love; let your soul understand that there is place for all. Do not forget that the world is afraid of one that has no love. Either runs away because of being scared or becomes the enemy and runs after you.

⊹══⊹

Those things that are secret come out with their adversaries. God is secret, because He does not have an adversary.

⊹══⊹

Everyone can give a piece of bread to somebody, but to forgive is the work of God.

What bad a fool can do its poition, hundred lions cannot accomplish.

⊹═══⊹

If you do not have a brain you are burned. But if you do not have a heart than you do not exist.

⊹═══⊹

The garden with flowers and greenery is provisional; the rose garden consisting of brain is always green and eternal.

⊹═══⊹

If the donkey would have been a customer and try to buy something, it will definately by the unripe melon.

⊹═══⊹

If a beauty holds an ugly with its claws, it means that it is ridiculing the ugly.

⊹═══⊹

To understand is to know, to know is to forgive.

Only those that have the same feelings can understand each other, not those speaking the same language.

—⊷⊶—

Gold's touch hides to unknown places.

—⊷⊶—

Love is affection without respect and measure.

—⊷⊶—

It is love and affection that humiliates the self and elevates a person. Without them, all the body is made up of greed. And greed is what lowers one. Love and affection are a human's rage and affection is animal's virtues. Be like a sun in loving; and like a night in hiding faults.

—⊷⊶—

I thought that the lover and the loved are two different beings. Instead they were one; I saw two instead of one.

—⊷⊶—

Love and pity are virtues of mankind.

Love, is the fruit of knowledge and understanding.

———

Being separated causes one to feel as if a year passed, when in fact, it was a winking time.

———

Crowds gather around sweet waters.

———

You see the way you look.

———

If mirror envied for anything, it would have been a nonbeliever like us and would not have reflected anything as it is.

———

The candles illuminate when the sun goes down.

———

A person's wings are his efforts.

Knowledge arising from immitation is the burden of our life.

⊹╼═╾⊹

The pity and goodness of the dumb are little.

⊹╼═╾⊹

The clever sees at the beginning, what a dumb sees at the end.

⊹╼═╾⊹

The enemy of a peacock is its wings.

⊹╼═╾⊹

Barley is equal to gold on the scale, but this does not make barley equally valued as gold.

⊹╼═╾⊹

You can renounce your anger, and God will take away his fury from you. What else could be for goodness other than goodness?

⊹╼═╾⊹

If it is not coming from inside of you, what benefit could there be of an advice coming from outside.

The death of one, whose life was sweet, will be bitter; there is no redemption for one's soul who prays for his flesh.

╌╌╌━╌╌

Do not think that I was working on worldly things when they will bring my coffin after I die.

Do not cry when you will see my corpse! My time of meeting my Beloved and reaching the Desired is this time.

╌╌╌━╌╌

These trees look like men under the ground; they take out their hands from the ground and make many signs to people.

They speak to whoever hears with their green tongues, long hands they talk about the secrets inside the ground.

╌╌╌━╌╌

Skies shake when a bad person, a cruel is praised. No one who is afraid of God will dare about this.

╌╌╌━╌╌

The pearls and Stones stay mixed under the sea. Things to be praised are within the faults and bad things.

If man were a real man with his flesh and corpse, there would be no difference between Holy Mohammed and Abu Cehl.

⊹⟩══⟨⊹

For our sake please be patient for a while; because patience is the key for happiness.

⊹⟩══⟨⊹

Ones own value is secured by his words.

⊹⟩══⟨⊹

Water is never afraid of fire.

⊹⟩══⟨⊹

Water has hundreds of virtues and magnificance; accepts the dirty and cleans their dirt.

⊹⟩══⟨⊹

The way of your life should not be swayed from the beliefs of Holy Mohammed. Do not leave Him! Trust your brain and capability less.

Not every wing can pass the sea.

⫯⫯⫯

Profit is only in good deeds and religion; the real escape in both worlds will be from these.

⫯⫯⫯

If you want to know somebody; look at his friends.

⫯⫯⫯

Mind is for thinking and taking precautions, not to be sorry afterwards.

⫯⫯⫯

A dog will not eat a bone or bread thrown at it without smelling.

⫯⫯⫯

If what you think is a rose, you are a rose garden; but if you think about a prickle than you are a block of stone.

If those that are religiously observant act lazily, the nonbelievers' rule.

⊹⊱═⊰⊹

Mighty God said that non-believers were dirty. But be careful; they are not dirty on the outside. That dirt is their religion and immorality.

⊹⊱═⊰⊹

The true dirt can be cleaned with water; but the moral dirt, the sins cannot be cleaned by water, and they might increase.

⊹⊱═⊰⊹

One who hits the rug with a stick, cannot beat the rug, he can only remove the dust.

⊹⊱═⊰⊹

Do not loose hope in time of hardship; work, show effort. You will see those sunny days, happy times will embrace you sometime. Hardness is together with easy times, come to your senses and never loose hope.

Do not go towards hopelessness, there are hopes; do not go towards darkness, there are suns.

⊹══⊹

The lowly in character, when they see pity, they will be sufferers.

⊹══⊹

Give to your friend whatever good you have.

⊹══⊹

A lowly person's enemy is heights; there is always a customer for eveything.

⊹══⊹

The colour of the face is the agent of the heart.

⊹══⊹

That allowance you give is a guard for your pocket. Praying is the Shepard of that allowance.

There will be no clouds, no rain on a nation, which do not give any allowance. There will be many epidemic diseases in a community addicted to adultry.

✦═══✦

The ideas of men are like birds flying in the air. They cannot be caught and imprisoned.

✦═══✦

If every sin makes one drunk like liquor, you would not see anybody sobre.

✦═══✦

One that speaks long is one who cannot explain his intentions.

✦═══✦

The biggest waste is spending life uselessly. Because, you cannot bring back one hour of your life by thousands of money.

✦═══✦

Try to plant seeds of goodness; you cannot get anything without planting.

It is not right to hold every hand; since there are so many devils around with a man's face.

✦═══╼═══✦

The size of hearts is the same in fact; but the virtues in them are all different.

✦═══╼═══✦

To mend a broken heart is much worthy than visiting holy places hundreds of times.

✦═══╼═══✦

A dog is more honorable and trustworthy than a person who breaks hearts.

✦═══╼═══✦

In our belief to hold a grudge is cursing; to hold our hearts as clean and pure as a mirror is our prayer.

✦═══╼═══✦

Book is a soul's food, and a mind's medicine.

A bowl is afraid of the stone.

＊━━＊

Do not speak badly; think bad, advice bad; than you will be saved from the malices of this world that might come upon you.

＊━━＊

If you want to live like a true Muslim, hold onto Qouran; because without Quoran to live a true Islamic life is impossible.

＊━━＊

I wish a mouth like skies; so that I can praise the Prophet so much that even the angels will get jealous.

＊━━＊

I am the servant of the Quoran and the dust on Mohammed's path as long as I live. Hold onto God tight.

Oh Brother, free yourself from Abu Cehl soon! If along the way of belief and obediance one is in a loss than I am a non-believer.

＊━━＊

Music increases the love of a lover, the grievence of a grieving, the happiness of a happy person.

Music is the breeding of those souls in love with God. Because in music; there is hope of reaching God.

My enemies send their dogs upon me. Those dogs bite me. I am not a dog, I cannot bite; but I can bite my lips.

The prickle is a beautiful three-cornered thing; it will hurt whichever way you place it.

⊹═══⊹

Exchange ideas with your concioussness in what you do and do the opposite of what it says.

⊹═══⊹

Everything breaks because of being thin; man breaks because of being thick.

⊹═══⊹

Can the mirror and the scale lie?

⊹═══⊹

A white and a black flags are drawn; one by Adam and the other by the devil.

Oh the young one! In this holy journey, to achieve your goal, put on your work belt and pray to God like the candle beside the praying seat, till the morning.

⊹══►══⊹

To visit a sick person is much worthy than a useless pray.

⊹══►══⊹

If the drunkenness of anything that is forbidden by religion were like the wine, the drunk and the sober would have been obvious at that instant.

⊹══►══⊹

One, who reads, understands as much as his mind.

⊹══►══⊹

Because of greed, truth would look like a false thing to you. Because of greed, hundreds of blindness keeps increasing in you.

⊹══►══⊹

The rat's eyes, which eat the praying seat candle, will be blind. Where is the wheat of forty years' servitude, if there is not a rat in your store?

Wine makes one indecent, who is already indecent.

Some men study just for fame and profit. These look like rats; they rampage everywhere but are unaware of the illuminance of reaching the desired!

Knowledge becomes with with mind, work with will.
Knowledge is minds, worshipping is heart's sustenance.
If knowledge is reflected to heart, it will be the lover of its owner.
If it rests in the mould it will be the rust for its owner.

Both kinds of bees feed from the same place,
But in one poison, in the other honey forms.
Both kinds of dears eat grass, drink water,
But one produces garbage, the other produces beauty.
Both kinds of canes get their water from the same place,
But one's inside is empty; the other is filled with sugar.
You can find hundreds of such examples,
But all two similar things are far apart and different from each other like a distance of seventy years.
One eats and gets dumb, falls far apart from Him,
The other eats and is filled up with God's light from head to toe.

Most people are man-eaters; do not be fooled by their smiles!

⊹╼═╾⊹

Human is small lenghtwise; but is bigger than nature and the universe.

⊹╼═╾⊹

Spending Money is an honour for a wealthy man. Love's richness is giving your life for it.

⊹╼═╾⊹

Nothing is yours, what is it that you cannot divide?
No life is yours, why are you fighting?

⊹╼═╾⊹

Jackals are afraid of the sound of the drums; but a clever person hits it in such a way that, you would not believe it is a drum.

⊹╼═╾⊹

Like water causing thirsty to be mistaken a true word cleans the heart.

Days that pass by without seeing a friend's face are like being asleep or dead.

⊹══⊱⊰══⊹

He is a friend, not garbage; do not break him.

⊹══⊱⊰══⊹

This world is a prison, and we are the prisoners in it.
Break the prison's walls, free yourself.

⊹══⊱⊰══⊹

World is a useless toy of holy, a precious swing of a dumb.

⊹══⊱⊰══⊹

How friendly he might speak, of what account he might talk, know that they are your enemy's words and that they are traps.

⊹══⊱⊰══⊹

Open your eyes and look at Quoran. All the sentences, which are God's words teach morals.

⊹══⊱⊰══⊹

One's knowledge and morals are his greatest values; they do not get old, they do not get lost.

We have seen so many people without their clothes on!
We have seen so many clothes with no one in them!

+≡≡+

To water trees is justice, to water prickles is cruelty. Justice is to place a value to where it belongs. Do not think that it is a good thing to water every root.

+≡≡+

Even if poverty and being in need scares met o death, I would not swap my freedom to being a prisoner.

+≡≡+

Most miseries happen to Prophets. Because to tame a dumb person is a misery by itself.

+≡≡+

Philosophy was very useful for me, but I am a couple of worlds away from it.

+≡≡+

Philosophy of a philosopher increases the suspicions and questions of men. The knowledge of Islam, causes men to reach a higher level.

A bath stone in the hands of a dirty man,
Does not increase its value even if it is made up of gold.

——

Everything that belongs to yesterday is gone with yesterday, my dear. New things must be told today.

——

Oh the lover! Wake up from sleep, take the pain! Is there a chance for a thirsty to sleep on a corner while hearing the sound of the water from the other corner?

——

No one can be a better guide than one's own eyes.

——

What can I do with an eye that sees far away, but not the traps on my may?

——

Wherever there is a river that place becomes green; wherever tears are shed that place receives goodness.

Lets come together and understand eacih other, because we will die suddenly, and we will fall apart.

‹════›

To be proud is a poison; when pride gets in your mind, you take as an enemy whoever breaks you; you will keep a grudge to who ever says a word against your ideas.

‹════›

Regular grass grows in two months; but red roses gow in one year.

‹════›

Who says that roses live in patronage of prickles?
The dignity of the prickle is only by the rose!

‹════›

Hurry spoils many things; you must do whatever you desire, slowly but in a secure way. Do not forget that God makes one mature slowly, in forty years.

‹════›

Which seed was thrown into the ground and did not grow?
Why are you suspicious that man will not reborn?

Can it be said that a seed dies, when thrown into the ground?

⊹═⊱

Know well that; an immoral but a beautiful face is worth nothing.

⊹═⊱

Mind searching for the absolute truth by itself, is like a donkey immersed in mud.

⊹═⊱

Imagine each of of your bad habits as a bush and that the prickles of that bush immersed to your foot.

⊹═⊱

Knowledge is like an endless sea without a shore. A person with knowledge is a diver swept to that shore.

⊹═⊱

There are so many scholars that are without the true knowledge. This kind of a scholar is only a knowledge memorizer, not a knowledge lover.

In the way of God there is no way for the mind's.horses.

<hr>

My God! There is nothing worst than being away from you. Everything gets mixed up and is a worthless effort. The only thing to do is retreating back to you.

<hr>

Everyone is happy when being freed. But I find the best satisfaction in being a slave of God.

<hr>

You can enjoy yourself today saying that I have money, gold. You never remember the day when you were in need of a single dime.

<hr>

Those lacking honour do not love their country and nation; we have to be careful from those people.

<hr>

One does not find fault in his bee, if he eats honey.

A bad snake only kills a person; a bad friend sends one to hell.

⊹⊱═⊰⊹

This world is a trap; and the passions are the bait!

⊹⊱═⊰⊹

One, who searches for a faultless friend, stays friendless.

⊹⊱═⊰⊹

We look like a breast with milk.
We give milk according to the hand that pulls us.

⊹⊱═⊰⊹

Prickle is the mother of the rose.

⊹⊱═⊰⊹

Those grasses you walked on today will grow on the ground tomorrow.

⊹⊱═⊰⊹

If you do not wash and clean your soul constantly,
Do not expect help from praying.

A lucky brunch grows from a good tree.

⊹══⊷⊷

A lover, within hundreds of people, is as clear as the moon shining between the stars.

⊹══⊷⊷

Oh from love and the forms of love!
Its' fire burned and charred my soul!

⊹══⊷⊷

A lover keeps his eyes on his loved one,
Does everything that his loved wants.
A lover does not forget his loved one; keeps remembering the loved one constantly.

⊹══⊷⊷

Whatever love has inside, it can be sacrificed to the beloved.

⊹══⊷⊷

Everyone passes through the animalistic love circle at one time or another.

You named lust as love;
If it were so, than donkey would have been the king of man.

Love will not get its lesson from any catasthrophy.

Those placing baits on fishing lines, do this not because they are generous; they do this to catch fish.

Anything other than sea is painful for fish.

Three things is necessary in life to be successful: attention, working and organization.

Be as silent as a book besides an illiterate.

If you see a person getting used to mosques, you will see that he is a believer.

✦━━✦━━✦

Be a sword over the heads of enemies of religion, spill fire onto those that are like Wolfes; because they are the enemies of the Prophet.

✦━━✦━━✦

Do not envy others; there are so many people that envy your life.

✦━━✦━━✦

The repentance of nonbeliever is worst than his sin.

✦━━✦━━✦

If a picture tries to throw a clutch to the painter, it rips off its own beard and hair.

✦━━✦━━✦

Be a word to be remembered well. Because man is made up of good words spoken about him.

If a bird tries to fly without its wings grown, it will be a morsel to a wild cat.

If you do not want something bad to happen to you from others, do not be a bad speaker, a bad teacher and a bad thinker.

The ugliness of a bad word is not from the letters; the bitterness of the seawater is not from the pot.

Everything is fixed by destiny. Accept it as your luck in order to be happy.

A greedy will not be thankful; he never stops being hungry.

If a judge accepts bribe, he will not be able to differ between the innocent and the guilty.

In times of need friend is the mirror of life.

‡‡

If there is no listener the music is a burden to a master. He will not desire to play or compose a new song.

‡‡

Fire is always freightened by water but can anyone scare water with fire.

‡‡

For one to see others' faults and mock about them is in reality seeing his mistakes.

‡‡

To be a sun and being like golden rays
I wish to be dispersed to deserts and seas.
Blowing at night and mixing with innocents ' shouts
I wish to be the face's wind.

‡‡

We are beautiful; you also become beautiful, ordane yourself,
Fill yourself with our attitudes, get used to us not to others.
Do not be a drop, become a sea
Since you miss the sea, eliminate the dropper.

Possesions and Money are like hat on the head, one wearing a hat is bold.

⊹═══⊱⊰═══⊹

There are so many birds flying in search of a piece of food...Their search for food causes their throats to be cut.

⊹═══⊱⊰═══⊹

A face like a rose is needed for reluctance. If you do not have such a face, do not walk around bad habits.

⊹═══⊱⊰═══⊹

Every blessing has a range.

⊹═══⊱⊰═══⊹

Parrot is the imitator. But man always chooses the good, the right and the beautiful. To be choosy is the most important virtue of mankind.

⊹═══⊱⊰═══⊹

Man sleeps; his soul shines like a sun in the sky. But the body is under the blanket. The body is like a rope tied to lives foot; pulls it to the earth costantly.

Patiance is pure but has a sweet fruit.

✦══✦

Patiance is a poison at the beginning; if you take it as a virtue it becomes honey.

✦══✦

Patiance is the key to freedom.

✦══✦

To tell a secret to a chatterbox is like putting water into a cracked pot.

✦══✦

A secret told to more than two people, spreads.

A meaningles word is a writing written on water.

✦══✦

To puse means, in a way respecting power.

If a Turk shouts, God bless, not a dog but even a male lion spits blood.

⚬

Even though I speak Persian my origins is Turkish.

⚬

How a bended shoe fits a bended foot, the devil's legends and magics fits into bad souls.

⚬

If life is a pouch of gold, night and day is a thief stealing Money.

⚬

Whatever you want to search in yourself!
There is a life within your life, search that life!
There is a treasure in your mountain, search for that treasure!
If you are looking for the walking *dervish*;
Do not search it outside of you; search it within your passions!

⚬

If our cup is small, we do not have the right to accuse the world.

A direct advice hurt stone.
A stone will not get green even thousand springs pass by.

⊹══╼══⊹

With one look steals the souls, that see,
Surely not even the doctors will give him medicine.
If they see his rose face just once,
Those doctors will be in need of other doctors.

⊹══╼══⊹

The elders hold the art of life in their hands.

⊹══╼══⊹

To whomever they teach the secrets of love, they would stich his mouth so that he would not be able to speak a word.

⊹══╼══⊹

An ant misses the entire yield but cares for just a peace of wheat.

⊹══╼══⊹

The *kebab* on the table of the spider can only be a fly.

Love never gets advice from a disaster.

⊹≍≍⊹

They asked Mevlana what love was:
He replied: "Be me and know".

⊹≍≍⊹

After crossing seven cities of love we were still in the first street of the first avenue.

⊹≍≍⊹

Honey is sweet in every mouth.

⊹≍≍⊹

Intelligence is a must; but for man, mind must be as much as to know that, that intelligence is limited.

⊹≍≍⊹

Is there an enemy to gold?

⊹≍≍⊹

For a loving man the best place is his lover's lap.

It is hard to tell the truth, not to say it.

✦════✦

Grief makes you call God in secret; therefore, it is much better than all the worldly provisions.

✦════✦

A prayer without grieving is cold; is not worthy; a prayer in grief comes with love and from the heart.

✦════✦

There are so many fish that feeling safe in the water is trapped to a fishing line, because of its throats' greed.

✦════✦

If a man is happy, it means he made someone happy; if he is sad, it means he made someone sad.

✦════✦

If you decorate the speach too much you move away from your aim.

Real morality is the beginning of sincerety.

Neither the river is repleted of fish nor the fish of the river. Neither the world's life is bored of lovers nor the lover is repleted of the world's life.

The baits you put in a trap is not accepted as generosity.

I make patiance the ladder to whatever position I want to reach.

The patient bird flies much beter than all the other birds.

Knowledge gives birth to love.

The worst kind of man is the one that does not love and is not loved.

A person's words announce what he has in his heart.

†———†

A hungry stomach is the prison of the devil. Because, the torment of gaining a piece of bread prevents him making mistakes.

†———†

First get rid of the rat than collect the wheat!

†———†

Even if your clothes are old, your hearts' should be new and clean.

†———†

Good manners are the mind's appearance.

†———†

I wished altitudes, I found it in humbleness.

†———†

A life without repentance is a complete agony.

Be strong without showing aggravation and be gentle without showing weakness.

⊹⊱══⊰⊹

If the yeast is bad
It does not recognize morality and good values.

⊹⊱══⊰⊹

People are in sleep; they wake up when they die.

⊹⊱══⊰⊹

One who gives without being asked is called generous.

⊹⊱══⊰⊹

A bad thing's strongest witness is our conciousness.

⊹⊱══⊰⊹

Defend your conciousness from greed.

⊹⊱══⊰⊹

Richness makes foreign lands our country; poverty makes our country a foreign land.

Visiting a lot causes one to feed up, visiting a little damages friendship.

Even if you receive thousand cruelties, do not make any to others.

The world is a mountain, and what we do is a voice. No matter how strong you shout towards the mountain, the echo is that much strong.

Greeting comes before the words.

Love is the essence of life.

Love is a tool that discovers the holy secrets.

If the drum is not played what is the missing part of the festivities?

People's union of hearts is better than the union of language.

※—※

To whatever people pray to, the life of that is also poisoned.

※—※

Search the ox's colour on its outside and man's colour in his inside.

※—※

Be like a musical composition, so that after you die, people will talk well about you.

※—※

Be a lover; choose love so that you will also be the chosen.

※—※

Love is such sovereignty that it does not have any time.

※—※

If an empty pot is placed at a spring and left there for forty years, it will still be not filled up by itself.

This world and the other world are like a man's two wifes: the husband angers one if the other is satisfied.

⊹⊱⊰⊹

It is much more beneficiary to try to talk before fighting.

⊹⊱⊰⊹

If you killed your own self-being, you have escaped from apologizing; there is no enemy left behind in the entire country.

⊹⊱⊰⊹

I neither saw one who disliked his own mind, nor one who liked his luck.

⊹⊱⊰⊹

A tongue's interpretation of love is illuminating; but love that is not spoken about is much more illuminating.

⊹⊱⊰⊹

The *Khalifa* said to *Layla:* "Is it you that, *Mecnun*, got destroyed and lost himself by getting in love with? You are not more beautiful than those other beauties!"

Layla replied:"Shut up, since you are not *Mecnun!*"

A good neighbour is better than a bad relative.

⊹═══⊹

A friend's punch is bitter.

⊹═══⊹

Friends of one with a sweet tongue, increase every day.

⊹═══⊹

All the rivers are flawing towards the sea; but still the sea is not filled up.

⊹═══⊹

You will eat your bread immersing it into your own sweat.

⊹═══⊹

There is no end to generosity.

To learn knowledge and wisdom is a must for every Muslim.

*

Some mistakes are installements of a victory.

*

If you are not sure about one's mistake, do not complain about him to the King, you might loose your life.

*

Mistakes are the doors leading to a discovery.

*

Every library closes a prison.

*

A house without books is a body without a soul.

A deaf person's ear does not hear, a fool's any part.

⊹⟫══⟪⊹

Books, which help you most, are those that make you think most.

Books are plants that never fade.

⊹⟫══⟪⊹

A book opened with hope and closed with gain is a good book.

⊹⟫══⟪⊹

Never in your life do something; you will be afraid that your neighbour will hear.

RUMI SAYS....

1-One who is not with God is alone:
If you are with everyone and without me, you are with no one
If you are with me and without anyone, you are with everybody.

(Mesnevi 1/1614)

2-Oh Son is free, do not be a prisoner of materials:
Oh Son do not be connected, try to be free,
For how long will you stay as a prisoner of gold and silver?
If you want to empty the sea to a bucket,
The bucket will only cover your needs for a day.

(Mesnevi 3/9-20)

3-Excessive love of materialism destroys man:
If water enters into the ship, the ship sinks,
If water is let under the ship, the ship sails.

(Mesnevi 1/985)

4-Worldly awareness is illusionary:
One who looks awake is in deep sleep actually,
His awakeness is worst than his sleep.
If your being is not awakened with God,
Your awakeness is like being awakened in a prison.

(Mesnevi 1/409-410)

5-This world is enough for a materialistic person:
For a materialistic person, autumn is spring, is life.
For him, ruby and stone are all the same.

(Mesnevi 1/2924)

6-Good intentions are like a rose garden:
Oh my brother! You are wisdom from head to toe,
The rest is made up of flesh and bones.
If your thoughts are like roses you are a rose garden,
If they are prickles than you are a prickle garden.

(Mesnevi 2/277-278)

7-A man's real feding is the love of God:
People other than lovers of God, are like children,
Man's real food is the light of God.
Is it right to feed him with animal food?
A superior person's food is highness,
He is neither a tool, nor a servant of a throat.

(Mesnevi 2/1083/1086)

8-Man is recognized by his friends:
If a bat starts to feed fom the sun,
It is for sure that the sun is not the sun we know.
If the bat hates the sun,
It is for sure that, the sun is a shining real sun.

(Mesnevi 2/52074-2075)

9-The symptom of God's curse on a man:
One with God's curse on him sees everything wrong,
God fills his heart with greed, hate and egoism.

(Mesnevi 2/2513)

10-Cry to God for your sin's to be pardoned:
With the crying of clouds the trees' branches grow and become gren,
As the candles cry they sparkle, and get shinier.

(Mesnevi 2/480)

11-Love of God is out of the boundaries of understanding:
I talked about God very little, I did not explain,
Otherwise my tongue and my brain would burn and get to ashes.

(Mesnevi 1/1758)

12-Love of God is higher than everything:
Nation of love is different from all nations,
Nation and religion of the'lovers is God.

(Mesnevi 2/1770)

13-An immature person is like a child:
One who cannot free himself from pride is not mature.
Men's fight is like cildren's fight,
All are meaningless, absurd and horrible.

(Mesnevi 1/3430-3435)

14-An arrogant person sees the mistakes on others:
An arrogant one, seeing the sins of others,
Starts to shine like hell's flames, and looses himself.
Accepts his arrogance, as if he is the guard of the religion,
He does not realise his bad habits, prefers arrogance.

(Mesnevi1/3347-3348)

15-Turn to God with desire:
Grab to whatever you do with both hands and with desire,
Because in good deeds, desire is your guide.
Be humble or indecent or hobbling,.
Turn to Him, listen to Him, and come to Him.

(Mesnevi 3/979-980)

16-Mankind lives in fear constantly:
Man is poor and coward,
Does not have to be afraid of the thieves, look!
Even though he comes to and goes from this world, naked,
He is always in grief, being afraid of the thieves.

(Mesnevi 3/2633-2634)

17-Materialistic mind, causes man to be mistaken:
Materialistic mind is a slave of feelings and desires,
Preventing you like a road barrier, from God's way.
Lives that follow the scarecrows from behind,
Even if they advance, they end up in graves.

(Mesnevi4/1246-1310)

18- Worldly tricks are void:
Tricks done for worldly gains are void,
Tricks that decrease worldly love are nice.
This world is a prison and we are its slaves,
We must breakout of this prison and free ourselves.

(Mesnevi 1/980-981)

19-Wisdom is a burden for materialistic desires:
Wisdom becomes my friend if it makes way to soul,
If it is a slave of the body than it is a burden.

(Mesnevi 1/3447)

20-My God! Make my mind, which is a water drop, a sea:
You gave me a drop of mind from your presence,
Make me reach your seas, free me from this dripper.

(Mesnevi 1/1882)

21-Woman is the light of God by giving birth:
Woman is the light of God, not only a loved one,
Her, being creative not only being created.

(Mesnevi 1/2437)

22-Everything is in motion with God's love:
The universe turns like a mill Stone,
Crying and whining night and day.
Since there is no tranquility in this universe because of love,
Oh my soul! Turn like stars, there is no peace for you.

(Mesnevi 6/911-914)

23-Turn towards moral food:

Who ever eat barley and grass will be the prey,
Who ever eats the light of God, becomes the Quoran.

(Mesnevi 5/2478)

24- Love of God is eternal:

Others' love transforms from one thing to another,
My love and my lover are not mistaken.

(Divan-ı Kebir, p: 1412)

25- What really exists is the loved:

Everything is the loved, the lover a curtain,
The loved is alive, the lover is dead.
One who is emotionless towards love,
Remains like a bird without wings, believe me.

(Mesnevı 1/29-30)

26- Cut the heads of those four birds:

Duck is the greed, rooster is the passion,
Peacock is a poser desiring for higher positions,
Crow is your self, cut their heads.

27-Wisdom is God's palace:

To be illiterate is falling into God's prison,
To dive into wisdom is entering God's palace.

(Mesnevi 3/510)

28- Good moral values are the essence of religions:

I, in this world of desire and search,
Have not seen anything better than good moral values.

(Mesnevi 2/810)

29- Do not be fixed to the ground:

Hide the blossom; be like a simple grass on roof.
Like sun, crescent and full moon,
Come and travel in the sky without wings, arms.
If you become a blossom, the children will break you, will walk on you.

(Mesnevi 1/1105)

30-Disrespect is created from inattention:

That moment is the one that I reach my beloved.
Arrogance is born always from inattention,
But respect opens its spiritual eye.

(Mesnevi 5/4096)

31-God likes humble men:
Be humble if water of grace is needed,
Than drink God's wine of grace and get drunk.

(Mesnevi 1/1940)

32-There is no worry for one who is near to God:
In life's path there are thousands of traps,
And we are like miserable birds with desire.
Even if there are thousands of traps in every corner in this path,
Do not worry along this path, if you are with us.

(Mesnevi 1/374-377)

33-The essence of being, is God:
Who are we; the breath in us is you.
We are mountain, the voice echoing is you.
Our being, our air is your present.
Our existance is one of your inventions.

(Mesnevi 1/590-605)

34-Run away from show-off:
If you become a morcel, birds will eat you, finish you,
Hide the pieces and be as secret as a trap.

(Mesnevi 1/1833-1835)

35-Man can be destroyed, his essence can not:
When you see my coffin, do not cry that you are separated,
Why are you complaining about the sun and the moon that is going down?
Since you watched my coffin being let down into the ground,
see also that I can rise as well.
Which seed has fallen on the ground and did not grow up?

(Divan-ı Kebir, p: 367)

36-Only a mature person can understand words about maturity:
An immature person can never understand how a mature person is.

(Mesnevi 1/18)

WHAT THEY SAID ABOUT RUMI;
THE MIRROR OF HUMANITY

Mustafa Kemal Atatürk: *Rumi* is a big reformist who adapted Muslim principles into the Turkish soul. Muslim, in reality is a tolerant and modern religion. The idea of turning around in harm a devine music, and trying to get nearer to God, is the natural expression of the Turkish genious and assertion.

Numani from Shib: There is no possibility to find the magnificance, holiness, braveness and poetry in any other mystical poet's works, other than in *Rumi's* poems.

Molla Cami: We are near the end of our lives; we still are at the beginning of *Rumi's* quality. He is the king of the spiritual world and the prof of this is the *Mesnevi*.

Muhammed İkbal: I obtained the joy of the Holy Being from the words of *Rumi* that constantly injected accomplishment. Let me read again with *Rumi's* inspiration, the secret book of wisdom. His life spreads flames. But, I am like a spark beside Him... *Rumi* transformed earth into chemistry; from my dust he repaired reluctances.

Prof. Dr. Hani Fauk (Pakistan): *Rumi's* poetry is a happy light in the untapped spiritual darkness. At the same time, his poetry is a source of peace in life's unpeaceul and chaotic periods.

Anne Marie Schimmel: *Rumi* is in general the biggest poet in the mystic world, as well as being the greatest Islamic spiritual poet.

Nabi: One who sees the book *"Fih-i ma fih"* knows that declaring *Rumi* is declaring God.

Abdulbaki Gölpınarlı: *Rumi*, as well as being a high scholar, a unique poet and a judge, was also a regular person with his ideas, words and aims.

Prof.Dr. Neşet Çağatay: *Rumi* being one of the best examples of the *Divan* type literature, he was also a talented thinker in mystic, religious and literary fields with his ways of opinion and knowledge.

Lois Doncet (French writer): *Rumi* started an illuminaing period for Islam. He searched goodness only in positive ways, opposed slavery and advised that everybody should earn his life with his own sweat. According to him, humans are free and holy beings. *Semah* is a symbolic description of his philosophy. With *Semah*, He means: "When you turn you see God. The happiest day for one is when you see Him, indicating the day when you die".

Aliya İzzetbegovich: *Rumi's* works are beyond ideologies and languages. It is hard to find another poet with his style that can describe as easily, the ant, sun, flowers and the ocean, avalanches and mountains.

Muhammed Ikbal: God laid in front of us a ladder; we have to climb it step by step.

Prof. Dr. Ferid Kam: *Rumi* is a sentence written by God. Everybody thinks they can read and understand Him.He is a sun for us that can be seen from under seventy layers or clouds. We, only from behind those clouds that cover, can see a bit of the area illuminated by the sun and not the sun itself; this way, we think that we see it.

Prof. Dr. Irene Melikoff: *Rumi* lived in order to melt every bond that tore apart human masses, that captivated human souls, and thus melting and bonding people in the fire of a unique being. He himself melted in that fire and thus made his way into the souls of his followers.

Dr. Afzal İkbal: *Rumi* was a unique light in his era, and up to this day, that light's glimmer is shining the same way, in the universe. The world's biggest spiritual poet, whose name spreads the wisdom's illumination and whose works are universal, is at this day glazing more and more.

Muhammed İkbal: *Rumi* with his glazing soul... Guide to the followers of love and drunkenness... His reach higher than the moon and the sun. He uses the galaxy as the cord of his tent.

Prof. Dr. Said Nefsi (Persian historian): *Rumi* is one of the leading figures of the Islamic spiritual world and all the rest of the world. With his vision, the height of his thoughts, the simpicity of his descriptions and the humanitarin attitudes, he took his place within the biggest geniouses of the world.

Marcel Schnider: The turnings of the semazens remind us of planets turning in space. With the musical rythm and with an increasing speed you can see the serenity and nobility in the manners of these *semazens* that are in a state of trance. While they turn, they seem to be a single body. This unity of idea and emotion gives them a spiritual strength. This way, they can free themselves from the materialistic problems of the daily life.

Ord. Prof. Dr. Sadi Irmak: The reason that makes *Rumi* a great poet and uncomparable in philosophy and ideas is that, he is a person that time cannot wear out. It is a rare case that a person is still one of the biggest figures in history after six centuries. He is a brain that resisted against the time's cruelty.

A. Scrima: In *Rumi's* system of ideology *semah*, is moving towards a higher knowledge, a bigger freedom and a deeper love. It is as if, the *semah* of the *semazens* all dressed in white shows us "the universe is saying amen to love".

Dr. Celaleddin B. Celebi: *Rumi* is an ideological and spiritual conqueror of the universe, showing the Turkish genious. This done silently a without any blood shed as well as being unique in world history.

Prof. Dr. Amil Celebioglu: If we get to know closely the true great people, we will realise that the fire of love of humanity is always seen in the Prophets and other holy people. Sparkles of those fires start small or big fires wherever they fall.

Aliya Izzetbegovich: *Rumi's* philosophy, his works and poems being kept alive for centuries with the same magnitude and force really give us pride. His works have conquered the souls of many people, both in the east and the west.

R.A.Nicholson: Mevlana died just couple of years after Dante's birth. But this Christian poet is well behind in reaching the tolerance and love his Muslim contemporary reached.

Prof. Dr. A. J. Alberry: *Rumi,* saved the world from a big chaos some seven centuries before. Today, what will save Europe is his works.

Maurice Barres (French writer): He is such a poet that he is lyric, pleasent and harmonious. He is such a genious that from him you can get pleasent odours, light and some peculiarity. For me none of the poets' live that inform us from the worlds of light, happiness and enthusiasm can be compared with the life of Mevlana. After seeing his poems filled up with *semah* I realised the missing parts in Dante, Shakespeare, Goethe and Hugo. One who is enlightened once with the light of *Rumi* does not need any other light.

BIBLIOGRAPHY

CAN, Şefik, Destegül, *Konya Metropolitan Municipality Publications*, Konya 2001

CAN, Şefik, Rubais of Mevlana, *Cultural Ministry Publcations*, Ankara 2001

CALIŞKAN, Hasan, Evrensel Sözler Atlası, *Nüve Cultural Center*, Konya 2001

CELEBİ, Dr.Celalettin, Hz.Mevlana Okyanusundan, *Konya City Culture and Tourism Center*, Konya 2003

ÇELEBİ, Dr.Celalettin, Hz.Mevlana'da İlim, *Konya City Cultural Management*, Konya

EYÜBOĞLU, Cansever, Altın Sözler Antolojisi, *Simge Publications*, Antalya 2003

EVA de VITRAY, Hz. Mevlana ve Semah, trans: Ass.Dr.A.Ozturk, *Konya City Cultur and Tourism Management*, Konya 2003

GÜLDESTE, *Konya Metropolitan Municipality Publications*, Konya 1996

GÜNEY, Asst.Prof.Dr.Salih, Özlü Sözler, *Siyasal Books*, Ankara 2002

HALICI, Feyzi, Mevlana-Rubais, Konya 1985

KARAKAYA, Tayyip, Güzel Sözler Antolojisi, *Nesil Publications*, İstanbul 2002

KÖROĞLU, Nuri, Hz.Mevlana'nın Irsadı, Konya 2003

LA ROCHEFEUCAULD, Özdeyişler, *Varlık Publications*, İstanbul

MELEK, Suat, Anlamlı ve Güzel Sözler, Ankara 2003

MEVLANA/CAN, Şefik, Divan-i Kebir-Semeler (4 vol.), *Ötüken Publications*, 2000

MEVLANA, Gökyüzüne Merdiven, *Om Publications*, 2002

MEVLANA, Mesnevi (6 vol.), *Ötüken Publications*, 2001

MEVLANA: Abdülbaki Gölpınarlı, Divan-i Kebir, *Remzi Publications*, 1955

MEVLANA: Abdülbaki Gölpınarlı, Mektuplar, *İnkılap & Aka Books*, 1963

MEVLANA: M.N.Gençosmanoglu, Rubais, *M.E.G.S.B. Publications*, 1986

MEVLANA: M.U.Anbarcioglu, Fih-i Mafih, *Cultural Ministry Publications*, 1974

MEVLANA, İnsanlığın Aynası, *Metropolitan Municipality Cultural Publications*, Konya 2004

MEVLANA, Mesnevi, turk: Feyzi Halıcı, Ankara1992

OSMAY, Nuvit, Düşünce Atlası, *Oncu Books*, Ankara 2000

OSMAY, Nuvit, İnsan Mühendisliği, İstanbul 2004

ÖZCAN, İsmail, Büyüklerin Sözleri, *Timaş Publications*, İstanbul 2004

ÖZCAN, İsmail, Özlü Sözler, *Erkam Publications*, İstanbul 1992

ÖZCAN, Asst.Prof. Dr. Mustafa, Refik Cevad Ulanay's Mevlana, İhtifaller ve Konya Yazıları, *Konya City Cultur and Tourism Management*, Konya 2003

ÖZMEN İsmail, Dünya Düşünce Antolojisi, *Saypa Publications*, Ankara 1994

ŞAFAK, Yakup, Divan-i Kebir'den Seçmeler, *Konya Metropolitan Municipality Publications*, Konya 2000

ŞAFAK, Asst. Prof. Dr. Yakup, Mesnevi'den Seçmeler, *Konya Metropolitan Municipality Publications*, Konya 2003

ŞAHİNLER, Necmettin, Tarihe Adanmış Sözler, *Beyan Publications*, İstanbul

ŞİMŞEK, M.Selahattin, Özdeyişler, *Zafer Publications*, İstanbul 1999

TAŞÇI, Mustafa, Sözler Hazinesi, *Düşünce Books*, İstanbul 2004

TÜRKMEN, Özcan, Özden Söze, *Alp Publications*, Ankara 2004

UNLU, Ali, Vecizeler, Öğütler, *Şule Publications*, İstanbul 2003

YAĞCI, Ömer, Düşünce Atlası, *Deniz Books*, İstanbul 1994

YALÇIN, Halit, İnsanlığın Ortak Aklı, *Kent Publications*, İstanbul 2004

YENİTERZİ, Prof.Emine, Mevlana, *Turkish Religious Foundation Publications*, Ankara 2004

YILMAZ, Burhan, Bilinmeyen Mevlana, *Nüve Cultural Centre*, Konya 2004